Latino
Americans and
Immigration Laws

Hispanic Americans: Major Minority

Latino Americans and Immigration Laws

Frank DePietro

Mason Crest

Mason Crest
370 Reed Road
Broomall, Pennsylvania 19008
www.masoncrest.com

Printed and bound in the United States of America.

First printing
9 8 7 6 5 4 3 2 1

Library of Congress Cataloging-in-Publication Data

DePietro, Frank.
 Latino Americans and immigration laws / by Frank DePietro.
    p. cm.
 ISBN 978-1-4222-2321-5 (hardcover) — ISBN 978-1-4222-2315-4 (series hardcover) — ISBN
978-1-4222-9325-6 (ebook))
 1. Emigration and immigration law—United States. 2. Hispanic Americans—Legal status,
laws, etc.—United States I. Title.
 KF4819.D46 2013
 342.7308'2—dc23
                        2012010522

Produced by Harding House Publishing Services, Inc.
www.hardinghousepages.com
Interior design by Micaela Sanna.
Cover design by Torque Advertising + Design.
Printed in USA.

Contents

Introduction

by José E. Limón, Ph.D.

Even before there was a United States, Hispanics were present in what would become this country. Beginning in the sixteenth century, Spanish explorers traversed North America, and their explorations encouraged settlement as early as the sixteenth century in what is now northern New Mexico and Florida, and as late as the mid-eighteenth century in what is now southern Texas and California.

Later, in the nineteenth century, following Spain's gradual withdrawal from the New World, Mexico in particular established its own distinctive presence in what is now the southwestern part of the United States, a presence reinforced in the first half of the twentieth century by substantial immigration from that country. At the close of the nineteenth century, the U.S. war with Spain brought Cuba and Puerto Rico into an interactive relationship with the United States, the latter in a special political and economic affiliation with the United States even as American power influenced the course of almost every other Latin American country.

The books in this series remind us of these historical origins, even as each explores the present reality of different Hispanic groups. Some of these books explore the contemporary social origins—what social scientists call the "push" factors—behind the accelerating Hispanic immigration to America: political instability, economic underdevelopment and crisis, environmental degradation, impoverished or wholly absent educational systems, and other circumstances contribute to many Latin Americans deciding they will be better off in the United States.

And, for the most part, they will be. The vast majority come to work and work very hard, in order to earn better wages than they would back home. They fill significant labor needs in the U.S. economy and contribute to the economy through lower consumer prices and sales taxes.

When they leave their home countries, many immigrants may initially fear that they are leaving behind vital and important aspects of their home cultures: the Spanish language, kinship ties, food, music, folklore, and the arts. But as these books also make clear, culture is a fluid thing, and these native cultures are not only brought to America, they are also replenished in the United States in fascinating and novel ways. These books further suggest to us that Hispanic groups enhance American culture as a whole.

Our country—especially the young, future leaders who will read these books—can only benefit by the fair and full knowledge these authors provide about the socio-historical origins and contemporary cultural manifestations of America's Hispanic heritage.

chapter 1
El Norte

A babble of voices filled the room, some speaking Spanish and some speaking English. Concha felt tired but satisfied. Most of the people she cared about in the world were here today to celebrate her birthday. As she closed her eyes and thought back over her long life, full of joys and sorrow, she felt a little hand pulling on her skirt. She opened her eyes to see her great-granddaughter Carmen smiling up at her. "*Abuela*, are you sleeping? We want you to tell us a story."

She looked thoughtfully at Carmen and the other kids, great-grandchildren, grandchildren, great-nieces, and nephews. After a moment, she said, "I'll tell you what my abuela used to tell me when I was little like you all."

The children pressed closer around her knees and she smiled. "We used to sit at our abuela's knee while she told us about El Norte—the North. That's what we called America. We were still in Mexico then, but my uncle was already here. Abuela had never been here, but she had heard many stories. She told us of a place where everyone who wanted a job could have one. Where there was always enough food to eat. Where little girls go to school. We dreamed of someday traveling north to this wonderful land. We begged for stories of El Norte. Like you now beg for stories of Mexico."

Concha looked at the children's faces, one by one. "Now you have all seen El Norte. Some of you were even born here. What do you think? Do you like El Norte? Do you like America?"

Most of the kids nodded, but some of them shook their heads. One of the older children, García, said, "I don't like it here. The teachers at school talk too fast. I can't understand them. I miss my big brother who is still in Mexico."

But little Carmen said, "I love it here! I've never even been to Mexico. This is my home!"

A Land of Immigrants

El Norte means "The North" in Spanish. For many Mexicans, it means the United States. The United States is to the north of Latin America. Many people from Latin America come to El Norte. Some come here just to work. Others come to make it their home.

People all over the world want to come to the United States. Some are pushed. Something at home pushes them to move to the United States. Maybe they can't find a job. Or there's a war going on. Or there are too many people around. Something pushes them out of their home countries.

LATIN AMERICA

There are lots of countries to the south of the United States. Most people who live in those countries speak Spanish. Some of them speak Portuguese or English. All together, all those countries are called Latin America.

Latinos are people who come from any Latin American country. They could speak Spanish. Then we can also call them Hispanic. Or they could speak Portuguese. Or English. Or even French. Those people aren't Hispanic. But they are Latino because they live in Latin America.

Some people are *pulled*. The United States pulls people here. People can make more money in the United States. It's pretty peaceful. There are jobs. There are good universities. Maybe someone in their family lives here. Those are all reasons that pull people to the United States.

People who move to the United States are called immigrants. That means they left the country where they grew up. Then they came to America to live.

Almost everyone in the United States is related to immigrants. Some people who immigrated here themselves. Other people have parents or grandparents immigrated here. Still other people have great-great-great-grandparents who came to the United States a very long time ago!

The only people who aren't really immigrants are Native Americans. Their ancestors have lived in the United States for a long, long time. Everyone else came within the last 400 years or so.

Immigrants come from all over. They come from Europe. They come from Asia. They come from Africa. They come from Latin America. You can find someone from every country living in the United States.

> A **policy** *is a government's plan of action.*

Immigration Rules

Thousands of new people make their way to the United States every year. But the United States doesn't let just anyone live here. The government has rules about who can and who can't live in the United States. All together, the rules are called immigration **policy**.

The rules are very complicated. They change all the time. People argue about immigration policy. One group wants the United States to welcome more people. Another group wants the United States to keep more people out. Each side has their own reasons for feeling the way they do.

There are a lot of reasons for letting people into the United States. The world is all connected. It's hard to keep people in one country. They

Immigrants taking oath of new citizenship.

move around all the time. The United States also has a lot of money. It has a lot more money than most other countries. Some people think we should share it with whoever wants to come here. These people think that people are people, no matter where they come from, and that we should all share with each other. People in favor of allowing immigration also believe that immigrants are good for the country. They do important jobs that other Americans don't want to do. They buy goods and help businesses make money. They bring interesting art and music and ways of doing things to America.

LATINO AMERICANS AND IMMIGRATION LAWS

But other people say that the United States already has all the people it needs. These people think that more people would be bad for America. Immigrants might hurt Americans. They might take away jobs from Americans. They might expect the government to spend money on them. Americans might end up having to pay more taxes.

Other people have worse reasons for keeping immigrants out. They're afraid of people who are different from them. Immigrants often speak other languages. They belong to different cultures. They look different. But **racism** is a bad reason for keeping people out of the United States!

The United States has created a system of controlling who is allowed to come to America and who isn't. People from other countries who come to the United States have to have

Racism *is the belief that people with one color of skin are better and smarter than people whose skin is a different color. Racism is wrong!*

Hispanic children growing up in the United States often face racism because of their differences.

This woman from Central America cannot simply take the bus to the United States. She must have a passport to cross the border into America.

A street mural in California portrays the diversity of immigrants coming to the United States.

a passport. They get their passport stamped when they go through the airport or cross a border in their cars. This way the U.S. government knows who is entering the country.

Immigrants don't just want to visit the United States, though. They want to live here. If you come to the United States for anything other than a vacation, you have to have something called a visa. You apply for a visa before you come to the United States. You have to prove you are who you say you are. A visa lets you into the United States.

A lot of the immigrants who come to the United States are from Latin America. They're called Latinos. They're the fastest growing group in the country. Some have been here a very long time. Others have immigrated in the past few years.

chapter 2
Some History

"Abuela, please tell us another story," demanded Carmen. She was always the most talkative of the children. "Tell us how you came to America!"

Concha smiled down at her. "I've told you this one a hundred times. You don't really want to hear it again, do you?"

Carmen and the other children nodded. So Concha began, "This was more than seventy years ago now. I was just a girl of fifteen, just a few months after my birthday. Our country had been at war with itself for as long as I could remember, but this year was especially bad. We had a new president who shut down all the Catholic schools, including the one where my brothers went. There was fighting all around us.

"My parents were getting more and more scared. They decided it was time to join my Uncle José in Texas. My father could work on a ranch with him there. Tío José had applied for papers for us to cross the border. For ages we had been saving any money that we could get because we had to pay fifty American cents for each one of us to go across. That may not sound like a lot of money to you, but that was a lot to us. We were lucky, too, because Mamá and Papá could both read and write. My grandparents could not get visas because they could not read.

"We took a train north. It was hot and crowded on the train. But we didn't mind because we were on our way to America. It took us days and days of traveling. Finally, we reached the American border. After Mamá and Papá showed the papers to the men at the border, they let us go across. We were so surprised that America did not look any different than Mexico. It was hot and dusty. But Tío José was

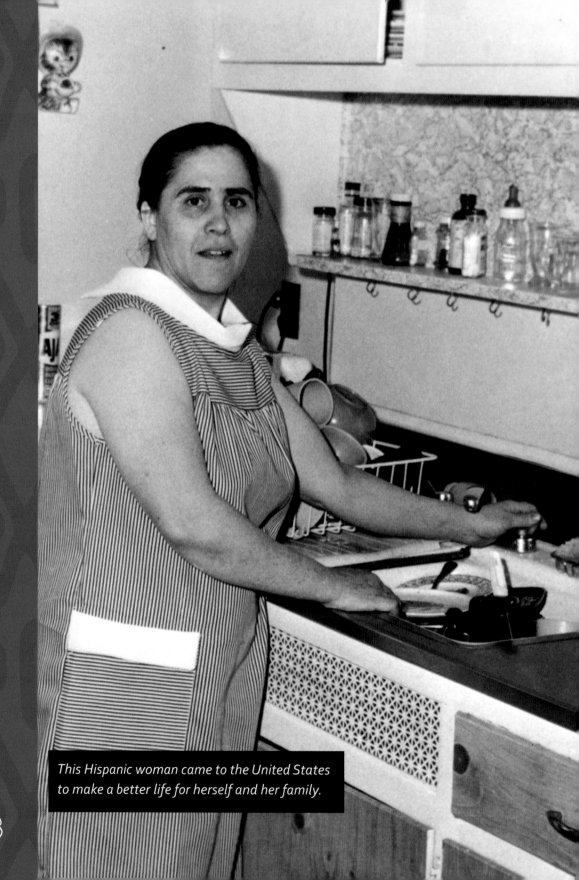

This Hispanic woman came to the United States to make a better life for herself and her family.

waiting for us. We all hugged and kissed and cried. We were in America!"

The First Rules

Immigration has looked different during different times. It was pretty easy for the abuela—the grandmother—in the story to get across the United States border. It's a little different today.

A long time ago, the United States border was easy to cross. There weren't any rules. No one had to have a passport or a visa. There weren't any police around.

Cities on the ocean had lots of immigrants coming in. New York, Boston, and San Francisco all welcomed lots of new people.

There were no formal laws until late in the 1800s. After that, some states starting making rules. Then the entire United States government decided that it had to take over making immigration laws.

President Lyndon B. Johnson signs the Immigration Act.

More and more immigrants made their way to our country. Cities started to get crowded with so many people. There weren't always enough jobs to go around. Lots of people were poor. Some people wanted to stop welcoming so many immigrants in.

A customs' card.

The government passed the first immigration law. It was called the Immigration Act of 1882. It made people pay fifty cents to enter the United States. It also kept out people the United States didn't want here. Criminals couldn't enter. People with mental problems couldn't enter either.

Another law was passed at the same time. It kept out all Chinese people. People in the United States didn't want Chinese immigrants. Basically, a lot of people were racist. They were afraid of people they thought were different from themselves. So they kept them out of the country.

More laws kept coming. They kept saying who could come into the United States and who couldn't. Pretty soon there were lots and lots of rules.

Some people had the job of making sure that the rules were followed. Government workers at each port collected the fifty cents. "Chinese

LATINO AMERICANS AND IMMIGRATION LAWS

Inspectors" made sure that no Chinese immigrants got in. Other workers made sure that other rules were followed. In 1891, the government started keeping lists of every immigrant who came in to the United States.

Keeping People Out

In the 1900s, the government kept making new immigration laws. It also started working on naturalization. Naturalization is the process by which immigrants become citizens of the United States. Congress passed some laws about naturalization.

A lot more people wanted to come here in the early 1900s. The United States didn't want to let them all in. Now Japanese people couldn't immigrate to America.

Another law kept out people who couldn't read and write. All immigrants had to pass a written test. That meant a lot of people couldn't come here. A lot of immigrants were poor. They had never had the chance to go to school. That's why they were coming here in the first place. They wanted to get jobs and go to school.

Now fewer immigrants came to America. Only a small number of immigrants could read and write. The rest didn't bother to try coming.

Then the United States entered World War I. Americans were worried about their country's safety.

The President said that all people crossing a United States border had to have a passport. That included American citizens. They had to show their passport when they went to Mexico or Canada.

After World War I, lots of immigrants flooded into the United States. The Immigration Act of 1924 tried to stop so many people from coming. They put limits on how many immigrants from each country could come. Each country got a certain number of visas to give out. If you didn't have a visa, you couldn't enter.

Illegal Immigrants

The only people who could legally immigrate to the United States had visas. Everyone else who didn't have visas weren't allowed in. That didn't mean that people without visas didn't move here anyway.

People still tried to cross the border. Lots of Latinos came to the United States without visas. They crossed the United States-Mexico border.

In 1933, the Immigration and Naturalization Service (INS) was born. The INS dealt with immigration. It was in charge of catching illegal immigrants and sending them back to their own countries.

The INS and Mexico worked together. They sent a lot of Mexican people back to Mexico. Some of them wanted to go. Some didn't. They didn't really have a choice.

Mexico's desert can be dangerous to cross.

LATINO AMERICANS AND IMMIGRATION LAWS

World War II

World War II began in the late 1930s. Lots of different countries were fighting each other. People from one country didn't trust people from other countries.

In the United States, immigration rules got even stricter. The government didn't want to let in people who could hurt the United States.

The INS had to write down and fingerprint every person who wasn't a citizen. They even set up something called detention camps. This meant a certain type of people were taken from their homes. They were sent to live in camps run by the government.

People who might be a threat were put in camps. Mostly, the United States sent Japanese people into camps. We were fighting Japan. A lot of people didn't like the Japanese. So the United States forced Japanese people out of their homes. They put them in big camps. The camps were dirty. They were boring. They were a lot like a jail.

Modern Day

In the 1960s, the government got rid of the limits on immigrants from each country. But that didn't mean America would let just anybody in. People now had to meet certain standards to move to the United States.

The Migration Department's reception desk in the 1950s.

Some History   23

Hispanic students in the United States.

REFUGEES

Refugees are a certain type of person who moves to the United States. Refugees are running away from home. They can't stay in their countries. There might be war there. They might be killed because of what they believe. They don't really want to leave home. They have to. These people are called refugees.

Refugees are different from immigrants. Immigrants move to a new country because they want to. No one is forcing them to leave their homes.

LATINO AMERICANS AND IMMIGRATION LAWS

People who had a lot of skills could come. If they were doctors or lawyers or computer specialists, the United States wanted them. People who weren't edu-cated or skilled weren't so lucky. The United States also let in people who already had family members here.

The INS focused more and more on illegal immigration. It caught people with fake visas. It built up **security** along the border. Now there were fences and cameras.

Deporting people became easier. Illegal immigrants faced harsher punishments.

September 11

On September 11, 2001, **terrorists** attacked the United States. It was a terrible day. Afterward, immigration rules would change again. Now people were more afraid of foreigners. They didn't trust that the old immigration laws could keep us safe.

New immigration rules were created. They made entering the country even harder. The INS was renamed the United States Citizenship and Immigration Services (United States CIS). It was harder than ever to immigrate to the United States.

But people still kept coming to America.

Security *includes things intended to keep people safe—like guards and fences.*

Deporting *means throwing someone out of a country and forcing them to go to another country.*

Terrorists *are people who use fear as a weapon to fight for what they want. They make attacks that are meant to scare people.*

The U.S.-Mexican border is more closely patrolled since September 11, 2001.

chapter 3
Who, When, Where, and Why

García spoke up again and said, "Great-Aunt Concha, was your Tío José the same José that was my great-grandpa?"

Concha nodded. García looked puzzled. "If he lived in Texas, then how did I end up being born in Mexico? Why wasn't my family in America already?"

Concha thought for a minute. "That isn't one of the happier stories I could tell. Sometimes the American government did things that weren't so nice."

Carmen piped up, "Abuela, I don't understand."

"Well, children, you've heard of the Great Depression? That was a very poor time. My father lost his job. Lots of people were out of work. There was no rain and no work. Businesses were failing People were losing their homes. People who had once been nice to us started to call us names and to hate us. They were scared and desperate. Tío José had worked at the ranch for many years, and the owner kept him working. But that just made the white folks in the area even angrier.

"We started to hear about people being sent back to Mexico. Tío Jose didn't want to go. But one day some men from the government came and told him that he and his family had to go back to Mexico. His youngest son, Juan, was a citizen because he had been born in America. But the rest of the family would have to go. Juan stayed with us, and everybody else had to board a train for Mexico. My parents were scared that we would have to go to. But we didn't. It wasn't fair. We all cried a lot that day." Concha sighed, remembering. "And that, mi niño, is how you came to be born in Mexico."

Texas

Latinos have been in the United States for a long time. In the 1800s, lots of Mexicans were living in what we now call Texas. That land was part of Mexico. There were thousands of people there. Eventually, Texas decided it didn't want to be part of Mexico. It wanted to be its own country.

But the United States wanted Texas. It took over the area. It made most of the people who lived there American citizens. This meant that they didn't go to the United States—the United States came to them!

The new American citizens didn't have a lot in common with most other Americans. They spoke Spanish. They didn't understand the U.S. government.

Colorful masks like these are part of the diverse culture that Mexican immigrants bring to states such as Texas.

LATINO AMERICANS AND IMMIGRATION LAWS

Latino immigrant in Texas in the 1940s.

In the early 20th century, many Mexicans wanted to come to America to escape living conditions just like these.

The United States took away their land. So far, American citizenship wasn't something these Mexican Americans even wanted!

Mexican Immigrants

But more people from Mexico would come to the United States. During the 1800s, though, there weren't very many immigrants from Latin America. Most people were happy where they were. The ones who weren't didn't want to come to the United States. They went to other countries instead.

In the 1900s, though, more Mexicans started immigrating to the United States. Things were getting hard in Mexico. People were poor.

LATINO AMERICANS AND IMMIGRATION LAWS

The Mexican Revolution was happening. The United States was richer. And it was close by. It was easier for Mexicans to move there than for them to go other countries.

A lot of Mexicans moved to the American South-west at the beginning of the twentieth century. They worked in mines and factories there. They helped build roads. They worked on farms. Then the United States passed laws that said all immigrants had to be able to read and write. Not many Mexican immigrants could. They were turned away at the border.

Then the Great Depression hit. During the 1930s, the economy was very bad. People lost their jobs. They went hungry.

Mexican Americans lost jobs too. But many of them hung on to their jobs. Other Americans were angry. They didn't like that Mexicans still had jobs and they didn't.

The government decided to send some Mexicans and Mexican Americans back. Tío José from Concha's story was one of them. The U.S. government broke up families. People were very sad.

During World War II, a lot of Americans joined the army. Mexican Americans and other Latinos did too. They fought bravely.

A young Mexican girl in the early 1900s.

During the war, there were lots of jobs back home in the United States as well. People were fighting in the war, so there were fewer people to work in the factories and on the farms. This time, the United States actually asked immigrants to come from Mexico! Someone had to work in those factories and on the farms.

Who, When, Where, and Why

Fidel Castro

Puerto Ricans and Cubans

Not all Latinos in the United States are Mexicans. Other big groups of Latinos come from Puerto Rico and Cuba.

Puerto Rico isn't a state, but it's part of the United States. Puerto Ricans are United States citizens. Puerto Ricans who come to the United States aren't immigrants. They can come and go as they want. Some Puerto Ricans came to the United States to look for work, and still do. Lots move to New York City.

In Cuba, it's a different story. In 1959, a man named Fidel Castro became the leader. He made a lot of changes in Cuba. Not everyone liked the changes. They came to the United States to get away from Castro.

LATINO AMERICANS AND IMMIGRATION LAWS

They tried to get here by boat. They were called the "Boat People." The United States didn't let them all in.

Later, the United States came up with a plan to bring Cubans here safely. They airlifted them in planes. At first, educated and skilled immigrants were airlifted here. Then poor and unskilled Cubans came. The United States didn't want them all here, so they stopped airlifting them.

Today, the United States is home to a lot of Cubans. Many of them live in Florida. Most are successful. They own businesses. They go to school. They own homes.

Dominicans

Some Latino immigrants are from the Dominican Republic. They're the second largest Latino group in the Northeast.

Dominicans first started coming to the United States in 1965. They were running away from violence in their country. Their government was changing. The Dominican and United States armies got involved. Lots of people weren't safe. They fled to the United States.

People came to America from the Dominica Republic to escape violence going on in their own country.

South and Central American Immigrants

Lots of immigrants come from all over South and Central America. Many come from Colombia. They started making their way to the United States in the 1960s. Today, Colombia is a dangerous country. There's a lot of violence there. People are getting killed. Many people want to get away.

Violence also took over Central American countries in the last few **decades**. People from Nicaragua and El Salvador had to leave home. Other Central American immigrants came too. They were all looking for better lives.

Decades *are periods of ten years. So the 1980s is one decade, the 1990s is another, and so on.*

Opportunity *is a chance for something good to happen.*

Culture *is the way a group of people thinks about the world. Language, religion, customs, holidays, and food are all part of culture.*

Today

It's hard to imagine just how many Latin American immigrants come to the United States. Almost one in every three immigrants is from Latin America.

Latinos still see the United States as a land of **opportunity**. They're willing to work hard to achieve their dreams.

Some people think so many Latinos in the United States will cause problems. They're afraid that our American **culture** will disappear. But American culture is made up of lots of different immigrants' cultures.

German culture, British culture, West African culture, French culture—all of them and many more mixed together in the United States. They're all part of American culture today. American culture is always changing. It's okay to add something new to the mix. And it's okay if some immigrants hang on to their own cultures at the same time. A person can be Mexican and American at the same time. Or they can be Colombian and American. Or anything else.

It all makes life more interesting in America! It helps make the United States a stronger country.

Three generations of Hispanic woman living in the United States.

chapter 4
Getting Into the United States Legally

One of the adults, Ana, bustled over to where Concha sat with all the little ones. Ana scolded the children, "Don't bother the guest of honor. She has lived many years and deserves a chance to rest."

Concha smiled and reached for the baby in Ana's arms. "Ana, I love my *niños*. I don't mind talking with them. It is important for them to understand where they come from and why they are here. Why don't you tell them how you came to be here?"

Ana sighed and perched on a nearby chair. "I don't know if I will be here that much longer. I came here to study at the university, to learn to be a doctor. I always thought I'd go back to Mexico to help my people, but now I don't know. That little baby deserves my help too. I just don't know what is best for her."

Visas

When Ana came here, she only was going to stay for a little while. So she only got a temporary visa. It was for people who weren't immigrants. She was going to go back to Mexico after she finished school.

There are different kinds of visas. Which visa you get depends on what you're going to do in the United States. Each kind of visa has its own rules.

Some visas are for students like Ana. Some are for people who are going to work in the United States. Some are for tourists.

Form to apply for a U.S. visa.

Usually visas let you stay here for more than six months but less than three years. A visa is often for a whole family.

Business visas allow people who work in other countries to do business here. They have to be employed by a company outside the United States. But they're doing business here for a little while. You have to prove that you're doing business here. You have to give a list of what you plan on doing. You have to show that you have enough money to live here for the whole trip. Finally, you have to prove that you permanently live in another country.

Then there are tourist visas. This visa is for anyone who isn't coming to do business or go to school. It can be for people who want to travel for a long time. Or who have to go to a wedding or funeral. Or to go to a doctor in the United States. It covers a lot of things. It's not always easy to get this kind of visa. You have to prove some things, just like with the business visa. It's better if you show that you have a specific event to go to in the United States.

Student visas are another big category. Lots of people want to study at American universities or other schools. First, though, a school or college has to say that it wants you to study there. Then you can apply for a visa. You have to prove that you won't run out of money while you're in the United States. You also have to show that you're going back to your country when you finish school. You're not supposed to stay in the United States after you're done.

Another kind of visa is the temporary worker visa. This is for people who want to work in the United States, but who don't want to live here forever.

For some temporary worker visas, your boss has to sponsor you. This means he or she has to apply with you. Your company has to agree to provide you with the same pay and benefits as American workers.

One common temporary worker visa is for farm workers. Every year, these workers come to the United States to pick fruit and vegetables. They live for part of the year in Mexico or another Latin American country. Then they come to the United States to work on farms to make money.

Getting a visa can be long and complicated. There are lots of rules to follow. It's easy to break a rule because you didn't even know it existed!

Some people want to stay longer than their visa allows. Then they have to go through another process. They have to get their green card.

In 2000, nearly 34 million nonimmigrant visas were granted by U.S. officials worldwide. The number dropped by more than 6 million in 2002, partly due to the attacks that occurred in the United States on September 11, 2001.

chapter 5
Staying Legally in the United States

Concha looked at García. "Why the sad face, niño?"

"I am thinking of my brother in Mexico. He would not come when we came. He wanted to be on his own. Now he wants to come, but he can't. My mamá says that it will be years before he can join us."

Carmen asked García, "Why can't he just come?"

"Mamá says that he needs a orange card, but I don't know what that means."

Concha smiled. "I think you mean 'green card,' García."

"That's right! Green card. Mamá filled out a bunch of papers to get one for him, but they tell her it will be years before he can come. I don't understand why it takes so long. I miss *mi hermano*!"

Concha gave the boy a hug. "Miguel will be here with us one day. For now, you just have to work hard in school and be a comfort to your mamá. She misses him too, you know."

Green Cards

Green cards let immigrants stay in the United States. These cards say that immigrants are **residents** of the United States. They aren't a citizen. They don't have all the rights of a citizen. But they can live here.

Residents *are people who live in a certain place. If you live in California, for example, you are a resident of California.*

Mexicans show their green cards to cross the U.S. border into the country.

Green cards aren't really green. They're little pieces of plastic that are actually pink. They used to be green, though. That's why people still call them green cards.

People with green cards can travel in and out of the country. They have to have a permanent home inside the country.

Do I Qualify?

Only some people can get green cards. And some can get them more easily than others.

People with relatives in the United States can get green cards easily. Only a very specific few people qualify, though. Husbands or wives of U.S. citizens can get them. So do kids of United States citizens. Parents of adult U.S. citizens can get green cards. So can adopted parents and children of U.S. citizens.

People with a lot of job skills can apply for green cards too. So can lots of other people. But there are only a certain number of green cards given out for these reason, so they're hard to get.

There's no limit to how many family green cards can be given out each year. But every other kind of green card has a limit. That means it's hard to get them. People have to wait for years and years, just like Miguel.

Waiting

Some people have to wait a really long time to get a green card. They can wait more than ten years. The waiting lists have a lot of names on them.

People who are waiting have to follow the Visa Bulletins. These are charts that the United States government puts out every month. They list the people who can apply for green cards every month.

Each sort of green card has a different waiting period. People who are applying for a family green card have to wait longer. People who are waiting for job-based green cards often have to wait less.

Staying Legally in the United States

chapter 6
The Law and Citizenship

"Grandma, cheer us up! Please tell us a happy story," cried Carmen.

Concha sat back in her chair and smiled at the children. "Do you want to hear about the day I got married—or the day I became a citizen? Those are two of my happiest days."

"We already know the story about when you got married," Carmen said.

"Yeah," García agreed. "And who cares about weddings? Tell us about the day you became a citizen."

Concha sat back in her chair. She was silent for a moment, remembering that long-ago day. "I was no longer a young woman," she said at last. "I had been here in American for many years by that time. I was married and my children were almost grown up. They were all citizens already, because they were born in this country.

"Luis, my youngest son, was the first one in the family to go to college. Carmen, that is your grandfather I am talking about. When he came home from college after his first year, his mind was made up. I needed to become a citizen. He kept nagging me until I agreed. By now, of course, I knew that America was not the magic place I thought it was when I was young child. I was nervous that if I didn't pass the test, I would get thrown out of the country. But I have loved America ever since I came here. So finally I promised Luis I would do my best to become a citizen.

"It wasn't easy. I had to pass a test. The test would have lots of questions on America's history and government. I never went to school in this country. I only knew what I had picked up helping the kids with their homework—and reading the newspaper over the years. Luis helped me study, though. I learned a lot. I learned about the **Constitution** and this country's Presidents and much, much more.

"I had to fill out papers, and eventually I had to take the test. And I passed! I was so happy, so proud. Then whole family came to watch me take my **oath** of **allegiance** to this country. It was a very, very happy day! Now I was truly an American. I would never have to leave this land."

Citizenship

Citizens are allowed to live in the country for as long as they like. They have all the rights that the government gives to people in that country.

In the United States, citizens can vote for their leaders. They are protected by the Constitution. This means they have certain rights that are guaranteed to them by law. They can't be **deported**. They can visit another country and come back to the United States.

Almost every person born in the United States is a citizen. People who aren't born here aren't citizens unless they go through the same process that Concha did.

Citizenship is the goal of lots of immigrants. Green cards and visas allow people who aren't citizens to be in the United States. But they don't have all the same rights as a citizen. Visas run out. Green cards can too.

Lots of Rules

If you aren't born a United States citizen, you can still become one. That's called naturalization. It means your nature—who you are, in other words—is changed so that you become an American. It's kind of

*The **Constitution** is America's written set of laws that tells how the country's government will work.*

*An **oath** is a promise.*

***Allegiance** is loyalty to something.*

*If someone is **deported** they are thrown out of a country.*

like being adopted into a new family. But in order for it to happen, people have to go through a long application process.

First, they have to have a green card for five years. They have to have lived in the United States permanently for all of those five years. They can't have left the United States for more than a year.

There are even more rules than that. They have to live for at least three months in the town or city where they start their citizenship application. They have to have "good moral character." That means they can't have been in jail for more than 180 days. It means they can't have been convicted of murder or theft. It means they might have done **community service**.

Hispanic people protesting unfair immigration laws.

Some people have to wait a shorter time. Husbands or wives of U.S. citizens only have to wait three years. Refugees (people who are escaping unsafe situations in their home countries) only have to wait four years.

Community service *is unpaid work that helps out others.*

How to Become a Citizen

So if you were an immigrant who wanted to become a citizen, here's what you'd have to do.

Some people feel as if it is too hard to gain U.S. citizenship.

First you'd go to the local United States Citizenship and Immigration Service (CIS) office. You'd fill out some paperwork there. Then you would hand it in.

The hard part then would be the waiting. The government can take a year to even look at your application!

Finally, the office would call you in for an interview. Someone would ask you questions about American history and government. You would have to prove that you could speak, read, and write English. You don't have to be perfect at English—but you have to be able to communicate.

Sometimes people's applications are denied. They can't become citizens. The United States CIS office has to tell the applicant why they were denied. People can have another chance, though. They can appeal.

chapter 7
Illegal Immigration

After her story, the little ones wandered away to play. Concha looked around the room to make sure everyone was still enjoying themselves. She caught her grandson Jorge's eye and smiled. He came to her and bent to kiss her cheek.

Carmen came back to her great-grandmother and leaned against her knee. She smiled shyly up at Jorge. She had never met him before. This was his first time in America.

Concha stroked the little girl's hair and looked up at her grandson. "Jorge, the children have been listening to my stories all afternoon. Why don't you tell them yours? Tell us how you came to America."

Jorge looked at the children who had clustered close again. "Bien, young cousins, I will tell you a story. About a year ago, I decided the time had come to go to *El Norte*—the United States. A lot of my family was here, and there wasn't much to hold me in Mexico anymore. I took a bus from my home to northern Mexico. I had heard I could find a man there to help me get across the border into Arizona. I found the man I was looking for. He was a young guy wearing a baseball hat and a lot of gold jewelry.

"I paid him $750 for his help. Many of us, mostly all young men, were put into a van. The man drove us out into the desert. We carried a couple bottles of water and a few other things in our bags. But that was all.

"The van stopped. Then we started walking. We walked and walked. The man promised he knew where we were going. I didn't know whether to trust him. But I didn't have much choice by then. We walked all day. Then it got dark. We kept on walking. My water was gone by now. I was very thirsty. I felt very tired. My legs were shaking. But I kept walking. The man told us that we were crossing into America now. I looked around, but nothing looked any different. But the man said we would be safe soon.

"I started to feel hope for the first time during that long, long day. But then I heard a noise. The noise got louder and louder. It was a helicopter. Soon, it was right over us. It shone a bright light down on us. I was so scared!

"The helicopter landed. We were surrounded by men in uniforms. They were all speaking English very quickly. They gave us some water, though, and I was grateful for that. We waited there in the dark with the men in uniforms. I knew I was not going to America that night.

"After an hour or so, a bus pulled up beside us. The men in uniforms told us to get on the bus. I noticed the man with the baseball cap and gold jewelry was gone. He had disappeared into the darkness.

"The bus drove us back to the Mexican border. Then it stopped. We had to get off. We were right back where we had started. After all that walking, after paying all that money, I was still in Mexico!

"But I don't give up easily. After a few days of rest, I went back to work. I saved my money. When I had $750 again, I tried again. This time I made it! And here I am!"

Crossing Without Permission

Getting to the United States legally can be hard. Visas and green cards are hard to get. But some people really want to come here. So they come illegally.

People who immigrate illegally to the United States don't have it easy, though. They have to find a way into America. They have to cross the desert. Sometimes they die along the way.

But they don't want to wait years and years for a green card. They need to come now. Maybe they need to make money for family back home. Or

LATINO AMERICANS AND IMMIGRATION LAWS

their families already live in the United States. Or the country where they live isn't safe anymore.

There are probably about 11 million illegal immigrants in the United States. There could be as many as 20 million! A lot of them come from Latin America. And a lot of those come from Mexico. There are a lot more illegal immigrants than legal immigrants in the United States.

Lots of Latinos want to come to the United States because there are Latino neighborhoods here. They can move somewhere that's sort of familiar. It's easier to move somewhere with faces you recognize and a language you can speak.

Illegal immigrants to the United States must often cross hot, barren land.

Latinos who already live here are willing to help others get to the United States. Usually, family members help other family members. That could mean helping them get a green card. Or it could be sending them money to cross the border.

Latino business owners are sometimes willing to hire illegal immigrants. They aren't supposed to. If they get caught, they could be made to pay a fine to the government. They could even be deported. But they want to help out friends and family.

Keeping People Out

The United States government tries to keep illegal immigrants from coming here at all. Over the years, the United States has passed more and more laws to keep out illegal immigrants.

The Border Patrol is in charge of keeping out illegal immigrants. It uses fences and walls along the border. It has checkpoints along the roads,

ARIZONA AND ILLEGAL IMMIGRANTS

Many Americans are very unhappy about illegal immigrants. In 2010, Arizona came up with a new immigration law. It said that all immigrants had to carry papers that proved they were legal. If they didn't have the papers with them, it would be a crime. Anyone who looked like an immigrant could be asked to show his or her papers. Police had to ask for papers if they arrested someone. If a person didn't have papers, he or she could be deported.

People were angry. Lots and lots of Latinos are here legally, or are United States citizens. They don't want to have to deal with the police.

Other people supported the law. They thought it would help control illegal immigration in the United States.

This is just one of the arguments that Americans have over what to do about illegal immigration.

where people have to stop their cars and answer questions before they can cross the border. Members of the Border Patrol go up and down the border. They're like guards who work to keep people out of the United States.

Border Patrol uses helicopters to help it do its job. It also uses high-tech equipment like motion-sensors. They work hard to catch illegal immigrants before they can get into the United States.

Getting In

As hard as the United States tries to keep people out, though, immigrants keep coming in. They always find new ways.

The man who helped Jorge get across the border is called a coyote. A coyote is an animal, of course, but this word is also used for people who guide others across the border. The coyotes know the land. They know where to cross. Alone, immigrants would be in danger. They could die in the desert. The coyotes help them find their way.

But coyotes don't help illegal immigrants just to be nice. They charge a lot of money for their help. And if people get caught trying to cross the border, the coyotes don't get them their money back. There are no guarantees!

Even with a coyote, crossing can be very dangerous. The Border Patrol watches cities and towns closely—so illegal immigrants have to cross the border in the middle of nowhere. They walk for a long time through the desert. It's hot and it's long way to walk. People die because they don't have enough water or food. Or they suffocate in the back of a van stuffed full of too many people. Sometimes they get lost. Every year, people die trying to get into America.

But despite the danger, people keep pouring into the United States. They want to come to America too badly to just give up.

chapter 8
The Future

The party was winding down, and Concha was tired. She had loved having her family and friends around her, but she was ready to go home. She pushed herself out of her chair. She went around the room, saying her goodbyes. She had special hugs for all the children.

After saying her last goodbyes, Concha started toward the door. Then she felt a tug on her skirt. She looked down at Carmen's little face.

"Abuela, thank you for all your stories. Will you come tell some more again soon?"

"I am always glad to tell you stories, *niña*. Someday, though, you will be the one telling stories to your children and grandchildren. Then you will tell them about the way it used to be when you were young. By then, I hope things will be so much better for our people. *Mañana*, little one! You will help make tomorrow happen."

Arguments

The United States has been a "land of opportunity" for immigrants for a long time. People from different lands have come here to make new lives. Those immigrants have helped build America. They have helped make the United States strong.

But America also has problems. People are out of work. Many people can't afford the things they want for themselves and their children. So some people say that the United States should take care of its own people. They say that America should spend its money on Americans. They believe that immigrants, especially illegally immigrants, should be kept out of the United States. America shouldn't have to help people from other countries.

The terrorist attacks on September 11, 2001, also made some people afraid of foreigners. They worry that illegal immigrants could be people who want to hurt Americans.

Politicians keep looking for a way to deal with immigration. Some want to let more people in. Some want to let fewer people in. There are a lot of arguments about this.

Guest Workers

One answer might be a guest worker programs. These would allow immigrant workers to come to the United States for a short time. The immigrants can work and then go back home.

Back in the twentieth century, the United States started the Bracero Program. This brought in Mexicans to work in America. They mostly worked on big farms.

A lot of the people who came with the Bracero Program ended up staying. They weren't supposed to, but they did.

Workers weren't paid much. Their employers could get away with a lot. The lives of Bracero workers weren't very good. So the Bracero Program was ended.

Instead, the United States came up with a new visa. It was for temporary workers. This visa lets someone come to the United States to work for a little while. Some people think the United States should go back to using a guest worker plan a little like the Bracero Program, though.

Amnesty

From time to time, the United States grants amnesty to certain immigrants. This lets them become legal

There are so many illegal immigrants in the United States, that it's easier to make some of them legal than to send them back. It would take a long time and a lot of money to find and deport all of them. People would be very mad. Families would be broken up. It would be confusing to sort out.

Some people who are illegal have been living here for years. They are fluent in English. They have jobs. They understand the country. Their children have been born here. There's no real reason to keep them from being citizens. They're already doing all the things that good citizens do. They just don't have the same rights that they would if they were citizens.

Latino protesters with signs.

In 1986, the United States allowed some immigrants to become legal. If you had been living here for more than four years, you could get a green card. Almost three million people did.

Amnesty also makes the government money. People who get amnesty have to pay. Each immigrant has to pay $1,000. That means the government gets money. Then, when immigrants become legal, they have to pay taxes. That makes the government some more money.

Open Borders

The United States does not have an open border. You have to carry a passport to get in or out. Some people can't come in.

If we had an open border, people could come or go whenever they wanted. They could go to another country to work. Vacations would be easy to take. People could visit relatives wherever they lived.

However, open borders could be dangerous. One of the reasons that our borders aren't open is because of safety. We need to keep out people who might hurt our country. We don't want criminals from other countries escaping to the United States.

Some people don't want open borders for other reasons. They're afraid that too many Latinos or other immigrants will come to the United States. Then they will change the United States. They might take away the "American" way of life.

But Latinos are already a part of the American way of life! America has had Latinos living here since before there was even a United States.

No matter what we do about immigration, immigrants will come. They will come from Latin America. They will come from other places, too. The United States has a lot to offer—and immigrants have a lot to offer the United States.

LATINO AMERICANS AND IMMIGRATION LAWS

Time Line

1492 Christopher Columbus lands on the island of Hispaniola (the Dominican Republic and Haiti).

1521 Cortes defeats the Aztecs in Mexico.

1532 Francisco Pizarro conquers the Inca in Peru.

1821 Mexico declares independence from Spain.

1845 Texas becomes part of the United States.

1846 Mexican-American War begins. New Mexico (which includes modern-day New Mexico, Arizona, southern Colorado, southern Utah, and southern Utah) becomes part of the United States.

1898 Puerto Rico and Cuba become part of the United States.

1901 Cuba becomes an independent country.

1910 The beginning of the Mexican Revolution sends thousands of Mexicans north to settle in the American Southwest.

1943 U.S. government allows Mexican farmworkers to enter the United States.

1959 Fidel Castro takes over Cuba. Many Cubans immigrate to the United States.

1970s Violence in Central America spurs massive migration to the United States.

2003 Hispanics are pronounced the nation's largest minority group—surpassing African Americans—after new Census figures are released showing the U.S. Hispanic population at 37.1 million as of July 2001.

Find Out More

IN BOOKS

Blohm, Judith. *Kids Like Me: Voices of the Immigrant Experience.* London, UK: Nicholas Brealey, 2006.

Fassler, David. *Coming to America: The Kids Book About Immigration.* Kemah, Tex.: Waterfront, 2003.

Haerens, Margaret. *Illegal Immigration.* San Diego, Calif.: Greenhaven, 2006.

Jimenez, Francisco. *Breaking Through.* New York: Sandpiper, 2003.

Silva, Simon. *La Mariposa.* New York: Sandpiper, 2000.

ON THE INTERNET

Facts About Immigration for Children and Teens
ctlawhelp.org/immigration-facts-for-children-and-teens

Immigration: Myth vs. Fact from PBS
pbskids.org/itsmylife/family/immigration/article6.html

Kids Discover—Immigration
www.kidsdiscover.com/immigration-for-kids

Three Recent Immigrants
teacher.scholastic.com/activities/immigration/recent/

Picture Credits

Alexskopje | Dreamstime.com: p. 38

Americanspirit | Dreamstime.com: p. 12

Benjamin Stewart: p. 16, 24, 25, 26, 36, 40

Corel: p. 14

Dorothea Lange: p. 29

Environmental Protection Agency, Charles O'Rear, 1941: p. 42

Hemera Images: p. 22, 28

Jenkedco | Dreamstime.com: p. 35

Juan Camilo Bernal | Dreamstime.com: p. 13

Library of Congress Prints and Photographs Division Washington, D.C. 20540 USA: p. 32

Photos.com: p. 53

Popular Science Monthly Volume 70: p. 30

Richard Gunion | Dreamstime.com: p. 47, 48, 59

Ryan Beiler | Dreamstime.com: p. 56

Scott Patterson | Dreamstime.com: p. 50

The Jesús Colón papers, Centro de Estudios Puertorriqueños, Hunter College, CUNY, photographer unknown: p. 20

The Justo A. Marti Photographic Collection, Centro de Estudios Puertorriqueños, Hunter College, CUNY, photographer unknown: p. 23

The Records of the Offices of the Government of Puerto Rico in the U.S., Centro de Estudios Puertorriqueños, Hunter College, CUNY, photographer unknown: p. 18

U.S. Information Agency. Press and Publications Service: p. 33

Waite, C. B. (Charles Burlingame): p. 31

White House Photo Office; to Lyndon Baines Johnson Presidental Library & Museum, author Yoichi R. Okamoto: p. 19

Index

About the Author and the Consultant

Thomas Arkham has studied history for most of his life. He is an editor, author, and avid collector who lives in Upstate New York.

Dr. José E. Limón is professor of Mexican-American Studies at the University of Texas at Austin where he has taught for twenty-five years. He has authored over forty articles and three books on Latino cultural studies and history. He lectures widely to academic audiences, civic groups, and K–12 educators.